SAVED
BY
HOPE

We Win When We Don't Give In

MICHAEL BYRD, PH.D.

WESTBOW
PRESS®
A DIVISION OF THOMAS NELSON
& ZONDERVAN

WestBow Press books may be ordered through booksellers or by contacting:

WestBow Press
A Division of Thomas Nelson & Zondervan
1663 Liberty Drive
Bloomington, IN 47403
www.westbowpress.com
844-714-3454

Because of the dynamic nature of the Internet, any web addresses or links contained in this book may have changed since publication and may no longer be valid. The views expressed in this work are solely those of the author and do not necessarily reflect the views of the publisher, and the publisher hereby disclaims any responsibility for them.

Any people depicted in stock imagery provided by Getty Images are models, and such images are being used for illustrative purposes only. Certain stock imagery © Getty Images.

ISBN: 978-1-6642-2316-5 (sc)
ISBN: 978-1-6642-2317-2 (hc)
ISBN: 978-1-6642-2315-8 (e)

Library of Congress Control Number: 2021902861

Print information available on the last page.

WestBow Press rev. date: 03/17/2021

CONTENTS

ABBREVIATIONS

The abbreviations for the translations of the Bible used in this manuscript are as follows:

King James Version: KJV
New International Reader's Version: NIRV
New American Standard Bible: NASB
New International Version: NIV
Amplified Bible: AMP
The Message Bible: MSG
New Living Translation: NLT
Easy-to-Read Version: ERV
Common English Bible: CEB
God's Word Translation: GW
New King James Version: NKJV
Contemporary English Version: CEV
Expanded Bible: EXB

PREFACE

The Bible states in Romans 8:24 (KJV), "For we are saved by hope: but hope that is seen is not hope: for what a man seeth, why doth he yet hope for?" I believe that we are saved or destroyed by either a negative belief system (or expectations) that we call fear, or by a positive belief system (or expectations) that we call hope. We battle daily for control of our minds, our emotions, our futures, and our destinies that, in reality, are activated either negatively or positively by our fears and hopes.

God has called us to reign on this earth as kings and priests (Revelations 5:10 KJV): "And hast made us unto our God kings and priests: and we shall reign on the earth." "And be not conformed to this world: but be ye transformed by the renewing of your mind, that ye may prove that what is good and acceptable and perfect will of God" (Romans 12:2 KJV). It is impossible to please God without faith. According to Hebrews 11:6 and Hebrews 11:1 (KJV), "Now faith is the substance of things hoped for." I have found people who believe God can do all things but don't believe God wants to do things for them. No expectation or no hope! They are like the children of Israel who saw God do great things but didn't believe God wanted to do things for them. Paul, in Hebrews 3:19 (KJV), calls that unbelief.

Satan's primary focus of attack on believers is to deceive their emotions and thought lives: "And the great dragon was cast out, that serpent of old, called the Devil, and Satan, who deceives the whole world: he was cast out into the earth, and his angels were cast out with him" (Revelation 12:9 KJV).

The enemy is constantly speaking into our lives to create his kingdom of pain, crime, and hopelessness. This is a kingdom where hurting people seek to hurt other people, thus creating a vicious circle of hurt/counter-hurt and crime/counter-crime. Many of us find ourselves floundering between the mindsets of self-limitation and poverty. Thoughts that serve to promote a feeling of hopelessness or the mindset of our young people are to "Hit a lick," or, "Laugh now, cry later." I talk more about these two ideas in "Self-Fulfilling Prophecy."

We are saved by our positive beliefs that some good is coming to pass. Hope is our positive expectations: "For we are saved by hope: but hope that is seen is not hope: for what a man seeth, why doth he yet hope for? But if we hope for that we see not, then do we with patience wait for it" (Romans 8:24–25 KJV).

Thoughts of hope drive out thoughts of depression and anxieties. Conversely, thoughts of depression and anxieties can drive out our thoughts of hope and positive expectations.

Working in inner-city schools for over thirty years, I have conducted hundreds of suicide risk assessments. Students with small problems who believed that there was no hope or expectations for their situations to get better score higher for suicide risk than those with larger problems but had hopes and expectations that things would indeed get better. The future of at-risk students with bigger problems and positive expectations was literally saved by hope!

Earlier I talked about allowing our thoughts of hope can drive out thoughts of depression and anxieties. Many inner-city kids have learned to be hopeless. (learned hopelessness). I ask them to; "be not conformed to this world..." (Romans 12:2 KJV). But to transform the world to be like Heaven! Don't let this world change you. But change the world. Pray this prayer. God's Kingdom come God's will be done on earth as it is in Heaven! Change must start inside before change can happen on the outside. Which is the driving motivation for this book.

ACKNOWLEDGMENTS

To my beautiful, loving wife, thank you for believing and recognizing the call of God in my life. Without your support, I don't believe I would have had the strength or patience to complete this book. Thank you, Gwendolyn Davis, for the hours of work you spent in editing. Last, deep gratitude goes to my two closest friends, William Hollins and Randy Snow. William, though we only talk or see each other two or three times a year, I truly value your friendship. Randy Snow not only served as my high school coach, but he also proved to be a true friend and mentor throughout the years. I love you all! I am who I am because of the positive impact you have had on my life. Thank you.

INTRODUCTION

> The three most important things to have are
> faith, hope, and love. But the greatest of them
> is love.
>
> 1 Corinthians 13:13 (NIRV)

We see how important faith is in Hebrews 11:6 (KJV): "But without faith, it is impossible to please God." And we have one commandment to love God and love people (Mark 12:30–31 KJV). But sandwiched between these two powerful, scripturally necessary things is something we sometimes overlook: hope. We can have faith and an unswerving belief that God can change our situations but not expect that God will do it for us. We can know God can heal anyone but believe God does not want to heal us or have no expectation that God will heal us.

Hebrews 11:1 (KJV) tells us, "Now faith is the substance of things hoped for." This implies you cannot have faith without hope/positive expectations. Your expectations precede your faith. Hebrews 11:1 in the NASB words it a bit differently: "Now faith is the assurance of things hoped for, the conviction of things not seen."

In Christ, "we walk by faith, not by sight" (2 Corinthians

5:7 KJV). However, we often create expectations based on what we see or think we see. In this book, I show the importance of keeping positive expectations—hope!

First Peter 1:3 (KJV) reads, "Blessed be the God and Father of our Lord Jesus Christ, which according to his abundant mercy hath begotten us again unto a lively hope by the resurrection of Jesus Christ from the dead." Put simply, we are born again unto a lively hope. According to 1 Peter 1:3 (KJV), we can choose to walk in this lively hope or not. We can look to the future with hope or focus on the problems of the past. I encourage my readers to have hope no matter the circumstances they are going through. My hope is that after reading this book, you will awaken each day with positive expectations of what God is going to do for you. All things are possible for God. I believe God wants you to have good things. If you read the book of Revelation, in the end, we win!

> Cast not away therefore your confidence, which hath great recompense of reward.
> (Hebrews 10:35 KJV)

"Let us not become weary in doing good, for at the proper time we will reap a harvest if we do not give up" (Galatians 6:9 NIV). We win if we do not give in.

In this book I talk about things that Satan uses to stop or hinder our hope! I'd like you to remember this acronym:

Hold
On
Pain will
End

TRUST IN THE LORD

As I said in the introduction, we often base our expectations on what something feels and looks like. Proverbs 3:5 (KJV) states, "Trust in the Lord with all thine heart; and lean not unto thine own understanding." I translate that scripture to say, "I trust in the Lord no matter what my situation looks like or feels like." We must be like Caleb and Joshua, who entered the Promised Land when nobody else would because they believed (trusted) that God wanted them to take the land (Numbers 14:28–35 AMP).

But if we hope for what we see not, then do it with patience and wait for it (Romans 8:25 KJV).

Strong's Greek Dictionary defines "wait" as "to expect fully: look (wait) for."

King David talked about waiting on the Lord in the Psalms. I believe David equated waiting with trusting God. I believe our faith is activated and empowered by what we say. But our doubts and negative beliefs are also activated and empowered by what we say. That is why Satan was so resolute to get Job to curse God. Job empowered his trust in God by saying, "Though he slay me, yet will I trust in him" (Job 13:15 KJV).

The enemy deceives us by showing possible negative

outcomes and feelings. Satan ultimately wants to curse our futures by bringing them to pass through what we say. Jeremiah 6:19 (KJV) tells us, "Hear, O earth: behold, I will bring evil upon this people, even the fruit of their thoughts, because they have not hearkened unto my words nor to my law, but rejected it." We bring evil by our evil thoughts. We bring evil expectations by expecting evil.

Job 3:25 (KJV) says, "For the thing which I greatly feared is come upon me and that which I was afraid of is come unto me." The thing I feared came upon me.

I try to say what Job said, "Though he slay me, yet will I trust in him" (Job 13:15 KJV). In other words, "Even if it doesn't turn out well, I will trust in God!" I encourage you to read *Speaking God's Promises: Changing Your World* as a way to speak faith to your problems. We give more glory to our problems than we give to God. By glorifying the problem, we indirectly glorify the author of the problem. I believe we curse God through our actions when we do not trust Him. I believe it upset God when Adam and Eve trusted what Satan said more than what God said. And I believe it upsets God when we trust Satan more than we trust God. "For we walk by faith, not by sight" (2 Corinthians 5:7 KJV). **We battle Spiritually in faith primarily in two ways. 1 Our Faith or unbelief is activated/empowered by what we <u>say</u> and do! 2 Fight using Love and Forgiveness! Fight the good fight of faith, lay hold on eternal life, to which you were also called**, and have **confessed the good confession** in **the** presence of many witnesses. (**1 Timothy 6:12 NKJ**) We fight Spiritually by our <u>confessions.</u>

Using the sword of the Spirit, which is the word of God. **Romans 4:19-20 (KJV)** And (Abraham) being not weak in faith, he considered not his own body now dead, when he was about an hundred years old, neither yet the deadness of Sara's womb: 20 He staggered not at the promise of God through unbelief; but was strong in faith, <u>giving glory to God</u>; **Job 1:21-22 (KJV)** And said, Naked came I out of my mother's womb, and naked shall I return thither: the LORD gave, and the LORD hath taken away; <u>blessed be the name of the LORD</u>. 22 <u>In all this Job sinned not, nor charged God foolishly.</u> **Job 1:22 (MSG)** Not once through all this did Job sin; not once did he <u>blame God</u>. King David a man of war said in **Psalm 91:7-8 (KJV)** A thousand shall fall at thy side, and ten thousand at thy right hand; *but* it shall not come nigh thee. **Daniel 3:16-17 (KJV)** Shadrach, Meshach, and Abednego, answered and said to the king, O Nebuchadnezzar, we *are* not careful to answer thee in this matter. 17 If it be *so*, our God whom we serve is able to deliver us from the burning fiery furnace, **and he will deliver *us* out of thine hand, O king. 2 Corinthians 5:7 ** "For we **walk by faith, not by sight** " We like the children of Israel that did not go into the promised land we also say what it look like.

Secondly, **Faith works by love Galatians 5:6** "For in Jesus Christ neither circumcision availeth any thing, nor uncircumcision; but <u>faith which worketh by love.</u> " I believe You cannot <u>love</u> if you have not really forgiven and released those who have wronged you. Also, God's Kingdom operates in **Love** and **forgiveness.** Satan's Kingdom operates in Hate and unforgiveness. I believe Satan is working overtime to get us angry to get us to Hate to build his kingdom.

Speaking to yourselves in psalms and hymns and spiritual songs, singing and making

> melody in your heart to the Lord; Giving
> thanks always for all things unto God and the
> Father in the name of our Lord Jesus Christ.
> (Ephesians 5:19–20 KJV)

We talk to ourselves all the time, even in our thoughts. I know it is hard not to trust what you see in the here and now. We read in 2 Corinthians 5:7 (MSG), "It's what we trust in but don't yet see that keeps us going." We trust God's promises. Saying we trust in God is the same as saying we hope in God.

Second Corinthians 4:17–18 (KJV) reads, "For our light affliction, which is but for a moment, worketh for us a far more exceeding and eternal weight of glory; While we look not at the things which are seen, but at the things which are not seen: for the things which are seen *are* temporal; but the things which are not seen are eternal."

We must not look at or focus on temporary problems. Rather, we must focus on the successes that will come from overcoming those problems. When I received bilateral knee surgery, replacing both my knees, the therapy and very painful exercises were challenging. The more I focused on the pain, the less I worked to get better. But the more I focused on the benefits (glory) of the therapy and exercises, the harder I worked to get better. The light afflictions of therapy and exercises have a greater weight of glory.

I believe the more we focus on our expectations of things getting better, the shorter the problem lasts. I also believe the more we focus on the problem, the longer the problem lasts. I have learned that what we need to look at is not the temporal issues of life but what God has promised. The best example is in Hebrews 12:2 (KJV): "Looking unto Jesus the author and finisher of our faith; who for the joy that was set before him endured the cross, despising the shame, and is set down at the right hand of the throne of God." Jesus focused on the hopes and expectations of joy of you and me as believers. He endured the pain of the cross by looking at the future. Jesus trusted the Father to endure the cross. We, too, must trust God to endure our afflictions and keep our hopes.

Romans 10:11 (NLT) reads, "As the Scriptures tell us, 'Anyone who trusts in him will never be disgraced.'"

HOPE NEVER DISAPPOINTS

Our hope in God never disappoints! I believe Satan is trying to create strongholds of believing that faith doesn't work. Also, a stronghold of believing that if you don't expect much, you will not be disappointed. But God's Word says the opposite. Romans 5:5 (AMP) says, "Such hope never disappoints or deludes or shames us, for God's love has been poured out in our hearts through the Holy Spirit Who has been given to us." I believe no one can stop us but us and Satan is working hard to get us to stop ourselves. Satan is working hard to destroy or limit our faith. I have seen how the enemy has been trying to steal, kill, and destroy people's futures (destinies) by destroying their expectations. With God's hope, no matter what the problem, we win—if we do not give up. The Bible states in **1 Corinthians 3:21-23** "Therefore let no man glory in men. For all things are yours, 22 whether Paul or Apollos or Cephas, or the world or life or death, or things present or things to come — all are yours, 23 and ye are Christ's, and Christ is God's.: The above scripture points out because you belong to Christ, all things are yours. If all things belong to us, we do not receive because Satan has created a belief system that we cannot have. God says you can have all things. Satan says you cannot have all things. Who is the one you are going to believe?

If Satan can control our thoughts and feelings—create a stronghold—he can control our decisions, thereby, our futures. Second Corinthians 10:5 (ERV) says, "And we tear down every proud idea that raises itself against the knowledge of God. We also capture every thought and make it give up and obey Christ."

I believe ideas that rise against the knowledge of God comes from Satan. When we accept these ideas as truths, it creates strongholds in our minds and emotions. We have to learn to take every thought captive to obey Christ. Satan continuously tries to conform our thinking to his worldly way of thinking. God wants us to "be not conformed to this world: but be ye transformed by the renewing of your mind, that ye may prove what *is* that good, and acceptable, and perfect, will of God" (Romans 12:2 KJV).

Romans 12:2 (ERV) reads, "Don't change yourselves to be like the people of this world, but let God change you inside with a new way of thinking. Then you will be able to understand and accept what God wants for you. You will be able to know what is good and pleasing to him and what is perfect." We transform our thinking by reading and speaking God's Word! We also transform our thinking by meditating on the goodness of God, remembering and rehearsing what God did in the past, and worshipping God. We have to guard our eye gate and ear gate as well as our taste, touch, and smell gates for they can trigger negative thoughts and memories.

God is the God of hope according to Romans 15:13 (KJV). God is the God of positive expectations.

According to the law of sowing and reaping and quantum physics, when we sow negative thoughts we reap negatively. In quantum physics, every thought and emotion emits either a positive or a negative frequency. Those positive or negative vibrations attract equal situations back to the person who emitted them. In other words, we get what we expect. If we expect very little, we get very little. But if we expect a lot, we receive a lot! If we expect bad things, we are most likely to receive bad things. But if we expect good things, we are more likely to get good things. The enemy wants us to think we will be disappointed. I believe the Bible: "Hope never disappoints" (Romans 5:5 AMP). Anyone who trusts in God will never be disgraced. Challenges in life come to help us grow in our trust in God.

Students with depression or anxiety often say they cannot stop thinking or expecting the worst. Asking them to hold captive every thought and feeling to subjection is like asking them to swim upstream. You work hard for little progress. But as soon as you stop swimming, you seem to lose the progress you made. This leads to greater hopelessness for many. A tool I use to help them is to have them make a gratitude list and say the things they are thankful for aloud. I ask them to feel the feeling of thankfulness as they read the things on their lists. The more they focus on the things they are thankful for, the more their list grows. Similarly, the more the students focus on being thankful or happy, the more they transform their thinking. Studies show our minds cannot hold (maintain) gratitude at the same time as they hold anxiety and depression.

I have been asked, "What if you were expecting to receive something and someone else received it instead of you?" I say there are two reasons. The first is that God has something better for you! And the second that you are not yet ready to handle it. God wants us to have the best. Sometimes we see things we want, and we set our expectations toward those things. But God wants us to have something better. We get upset, thinking our expectations are unfulfilled. The reality is that God is giving us an upgrade. I have counseled women who were married but without children. Their expectation was to birth children, but God had other plans for them. They adopted children who gave them feelings of fulfillment and completeness.

I once applied for a job for which I was more qualified than the other applicants. When I did not get it, I blamed others. Even though I knew when you blame others, you give away your power to control the situation because someone else is responsible for where you are in life. I got angry at the place for not hiring me. I asked God, "Why didn't I get hired?" Years later, that same place had a large scandal, and everyone there was fired. Then I thanked God they didn't hire me.

The worst thing you can do is to give someone something that person is not ready to handle. I wanted to give my son a car when he was in high school, but at the time, he could not be trusted with that responsibility. One of the most powerful revelations God has shown me is that He wants us to grow up by learning to trust Him. A good example of this is found in Galatians 4:1–6 (MSG), where it begins,

Let me show you the implications of this: (1) As long as the heir is a minor, he has no advantage over the slave although, legally, he owns the entire inheritance; (2) He is subject to tutors and administrators until whatever date the father has set for emancipation; (3) That is the way it is with us; when we were minors, we were just like slaves ordered around by simple instructions (the tutors and administrators of this world), with no say in the conduct of our own lives; (4) When the time arrived that was set by God the Father, God sent his Son, born among us of a woman, born under the conditions of the law so that he might redeem those of us who have been kidnapped by the law; (5) We have been set free to experience our rightful heritage; (6) You can tell for sure that you are now fully adopted as his own children because God sent the Spirit of his Son into our lives and we cry out, "Papa! Father! Doesn't that privilege of an intimate conversation with God make it plain that you are not a slave, but a child? And if you are a child, you're also an heir, with complete access to the inheritance."

We as heirs; although we legally own the entire inheritance, we are not mature enough to handle it. In the natural, if heirs to the throne in any kingdom have a temper tantrum—is a slave to impulses—that person will not be trusted to conduct the affairs of the kingdom. God wants us to grow up so that we can fulfill Jesus's prayer for God's kingdom to come and for God's will to be done on earth as it is in heaven. God wants us to grow up and change our thinking to that of kings and queens and no longer think like slaves.

I once was eating dinner with a large church party after a church service. I sat across from a young couple and their one-year-old daughter. When the daughter was with her mother, they wrestled over the food. When she was in her mother's lap, they had a tug-of-war over a small bowl of fruit. She was being fussy. The mother continued to push the bowl away, wanting her daughter to eat one piece at a time. But the daughter wanted to eat with both hands full of fruit. The mother wanted her to slow down. I saw her later in her father's lap. The father was blowing on her food to cool it. The daughter was sitting quietly and looking patiently at her father as he blew on her food. She waited patiently for ten or more blows. I first thought she was conditioned to wait by the blowing. But God said to me that she had learned to trust her father. Both parents wanted her to grow up so that they could give her more. The mother was pulling away the bowl to keep her from choking on her food. The father wanted to teach his daughter to cool her own food.

God wants us to grow to trust Him and wait patiently for Him to give us stuff we are not ready for. If you had a young child, you would not give your child a loaded gun as a toy. God has shown me that trust is a two-way street. The more we trust God, the more God can entrust to us. I remember disagreeing with my wife. Later, I was talking to God, telling Him how wrong she was and how right I was. God reminded me of the little girl struggling in her mother's arms. Then God said to me, "You are being fussy." We, like the daughter, need to learn to trust our heavenly Father and wait patiently for Him to cool things—get it ready for us to handle. When we trust God, we will say no to our will and yes to God's will.

As I thought about it, I realized that I wanted God to change my wife, but God wanted me to trust Him in that situation. The more we trust God, the more we grow. The more we grow and trust God, the more God entrusts to us and gives us our expectations. Maturity does not come with age; maturity comes with responsibility. We become responsible by doing for others. When we are selfish and self-centered, God cannot give us what we are hoping for. God will not give us something we are not mature enough or ready for.

We live in a narcissistic world. People are only concerned about themselves and those who benefit them—family. Jeremiah 29:11 (NIV) tells us, "'For I know the plans I have for you,' declares the Lord, 'plans to prosper you and not to harm you; plans to give you hope and a future.'" In other words, God wants to prosper us and give us our hopes. We mature when we trust God and crucify our desires.

No one can stop you but you. Satan continues to try to get us to give up. He makes us think our expectations will not become realities, so we get disappointed. But in God, hope never disappoints. We read in Hebrews 12:2 (KJV), "for the joy that was set before him endured the cross, despising the shame, and is set down at the right hand of the throne of God." However, before His death on the cross, Jesus prayed to take this cup from me, but because He trusted in the Father, he said, "not my will but your will be done" (Luke

22:42, KJV). Psalm 37:4 (KJV) tells us to "Delight thyself also in the Lord: and He shall give thee the desires of thine heart." When we delight in what God wants, we want more of what God wants than what we want. Our expectations become what God expects, and our hope in God is *never* disappointed. Pray this prayer aloud: "Father ... nevertheless not my will, but thine will be done" (Luke 22:42, KJV). When we want what God wants for us, we will never be disappointed!

"For in Jesus Christ neither circumcision availeth any thing, nor uncircumcision; but faith which worketh by love" (Galatians 5:6, KJV). Our faith works by love. Our faith will not work when we have hate and anger in our hearts. Faith and hope only operate in love. Jesus said in Luke 18:8 (KJV), "I tell you that he will avenge them speedily. Nevertheless when the Son of man cometh, shall he find faith on the earth?" God will avenge us. We see some protesters angrily trying to get revenge by looting. God will avenge His people, but we must continue to walk in love.

LOOK UP

The Bible talks about looking up. In Psalm 5:3 (KJV) we find, "My voice shalt thou hear in the morning, O Lord; in the morning will I direct my prayer unto thee, and will look up." I translate it as, "Wait expectantly," in that looking up is waiting expectantly. Also in Psalm 121:1 (KJV), "I will lift up mine eyes unto the hills, from whence cometh my help." Jesus said in the last days in Luke 21:28 (KJV), "And when these things begin to come to pass, then look up, and lift up your heads; for your redemption draweth nigh."

During a therapists' conference, I heard a speaker talk about the power of body posture, in particular, looking up. Looking up empowers and reinforces one's positive expectations (hope). Looking down empowers our negative feelings. Looking down reinforces the belief that things are bad, creating negative expectations (hopelessness). I believe looking up helps us to trust God. I watch boxing, and one of the things I have noticed is that if boxers sitting in their corners looking down, they believe that they will lose the fight. Looking down sends a message that you are about to give up. I believe we win in the end if we do not give up. I ask my students to look up because when you look down, it sends a subliminal message that things will not get better. When you claim to have hope but continue to look down, you will believe what you do more than what you say. In sports we hear coaches say, "Keep your head up!" I say to my readers to keep your heads up and look up!

KEEP YOUR HEAD UP

You have to believe and say to yourself, "Weeping may endure for a night, but joy cometh in the morning" (Psalm 30:5, KJV). You can do some things to keep hope alive.

Proverbs 11:17 (MSG) tell us, "When you're kind to others, you help yourself; when you're cruel to others, you hurt yourself." In Proverbs 11:25 (MSG), we're advised, "The one who blesses others is abundantly blessed; those who help others are helped."

Psychological studies have shown that by helping others, you help yourself. They have studied depressed people and found that those who helped others were less depressed after doing so. According to some scientific studies, a chemical reaction occurs in the brain that makes you feel good when you help others.

I believe everyone can help others. We have to overcome our self-serving mindsets, the belief that we must promote ourselves and do things only for ourselves. My fraternity, of which Dr. Martin Luther King Jr. is a member, has as its mantra, "First of All, Servants of All, We Shall Transcend All." I believe we must put others first by helping them. Then and only then can we become great—transcend all.

I call this the law of blessing and cursing. Psalm 109:17–18 (KJV) says, "As he loved cursing, so let it come unto him: as he delighted not in blessing, so let it be far from him. As he clothed himself with cursing like as with his garment, so let it come into his bowels like water." When we bless and encourage others, we bless and encourage ourselves. The law of sowing and reaping, found in Galatians 6:7 (KJV), says, "Be not deceived; God is not mocked: for whatsoever a man soweth, that shall he also reap."

When we sow ill words and thoughts—cursing or putdowns of others—we reap cursing or putdowns from others. As a counselor, I'm always watching the client's body language. I have been asked, "Are you reading my mind?" I can't read minds. And I don't believe Satan can read minds, but he can read body language. Satan responds to the messages we give through body language. So keep your head up!

IMAGINE YOUR HOPES: POSITIVE EXPECTATIONS

"Where there is no vision, the people perish: but he that keepeth the law, happy is he" (Proverbs 29:18 KJV). The word "vision" in *Strong's Hebrew Dictionary* is *khaw-zone* (or *chazon*), a sight (mentally), that is, a dream, revelation. One's mental sight is the imagination. Where there is no mental image or mental vision, people perish. In the Orthodox Jewish Bible it reads, "Where there is no chazon (prophetic vision), the people cast off restraint [i.e., perish ungovernable], but he that is shomer over the torah, happy is he." When I was recovering from replacing both knees, I imagined myself walking, running, and jumping. I dreamed of running up hills. I felt good with no pain in the dream.

Many times we imagine the worst. Jeremiah 6:19 (KJV) reads, "Hear, O earth: behold, I will bring evil upon this people, even the fruit of their thoughts, because they have not hearkened unto my words, nor to my law, but rejected it." Our words, combined with our imaginations, can be a powerful tool for good or evil. People perish when they believe things will not get better.

In the chapter, "The Battle Is for Our Thoughts and Emotions," I wrote about Satan trying to create a mindset (belief system) of hopelessness. I found that we win when we do not give in. The best example is a story about a boxer in a fifteen-round boxing match being knocked down in each round. His coaching corner kept telling him to stay down, but after each knockdown, the boxer got back up. In the last round, he knocked out his opponent. After the fight, people asked what kept him going Why didn't he stay down as his corner requested? He answered, "I kept remembering a dream I had of me standing over him with the referee holding my hand up as the winner!" We, too, can do the seemingly impossible. But many times we, like Peter walking on the water, look at the circumstances (wind and rain) and become overwhelmed (Matthew 14:30, KJV). Many times we quit and give up on the vision—mental image—that God has given us. Thus the subtitle of this book: *We Win If We Do Not Give In.*

OVERCOMING DOUBTS

The Bible says in James 1:6–8 (NIV),

> But when you ask, you must believe and not doubt, because the one who doubts is like a wave of the sea, blown and tossed by the wind. That person should not expect to receive anything from the Lord. Such a person is double-minded and unstable in all they do.

We can ask with no expectations and not receive from God. God wants us to get to the point where we have positive expectations and hopes. When we trust in God, we know and experience that God has done it before and that He can do it again. We learn to have patience. We learn to trust. This gives us experience that leads us to positive expectations because He did it before, and He will do it again.

To have hope in God, we must overcome our doubts. I believe the enemy—Satan, the devil—is working overtime to create doubts in our minds to destroy our faith, thereby demolishing our worship. Revelation 12:11 (KJV) reads, "And they overcame him by the blood of the Lamb, and by the word of their testimony, and they loved not their lives unto the death." "They" in this verse are us, we overcome;

and "him" in this verse is the devil. In other words, we overcame by what Jesus did on the cross, by what we said (testimony), and by our willingness to die for Christ. We overcome doubts by what we say to ourselves.

Students with depression and/or anxiety come to my office feeling like they can't stop thinking negative thoughts. I ask them to imagine an elephant and tell them that whatever they do, not to let the image of the elephant disappear. I ask them to focus on its trunk, the gray color, and the roughness of its skin. I then ask them to say their names aloud—and loudly. Next I ask what happened to the elephant when they said their names. They respond that it disappeared. I then tell them that what they say aloud has more power than what they think. Death and life are in the power of the tongue! This is found in Proverbs 18:21 (KJV). We overcome our negative thoughts by the blood of Jesus and the words of our testimony, what we say. We should say, "God did it before; God will do it again. God did it for them; He will do it for me."

First Corinthians 10:11 (KJV) expresses, "Now all these things happened unto them, for example: and they are written for our admonition, upon whom the ends of the world are come." I used to say our mouths are the guns, and the words spoken from God's Word are the ammunition—the bullets. Now I say our mouths are the missile launchers, and our words are the missiles. We are not just killing our enemy; we are destroying all the works of the enemy. We can have the best weapon but no ammunition, which leaves us defenseless. We should ask, "Didn't you once dry up the sea, the powerful waters of the deep, and then make the bottom of the ocean a road for the redeemed to walk across?" (Isaiah 51:10 MSG).

I believe Abraham is the best example of hope in a hopeless situation. Romans 4:18 (CEB) tells us, "When it was beyond hope, he had faith in the hope that he would become the father of many nations, in keeping with the promise God spoke to him: That's how many descendants you will have." Romans 4:19–20 (KJV) declares, "And being not weak in faith, he considered not his own body now dead, when he was about a hundred years old, neither yet the deadness of Sara's womb: He staggered not at the promise of God through unbelief; but was strong in faith, giving glory to God." Abraham said or sang aloud what God was going to do. The more Abraham hoped in God, the more his trust grew. Abraham was also rich, and God bragged on him. The Bible speaks of his faith in God. I believe his faith and expectations grew as his trust in God grew; he trusted God for more and more.

I use these examples as my admonitions, God did it before; God will do it again. And God will do the same for me! First Corinthians 10:10–11 (KJV) reads, "Neither murmur ye, as some of them also murmured, and were destroyed of the destroyer. Now all these things happened unto them for examples: and they are written for our admonition, upon whom the ends of the world come." Overcoming doubt is in the power of what we say. In Psalm 5:3 (NIV) King David said, "In the morning, Lord, you hear my voice; in the morning I lay my requests before you and wait expectantly." God hears our voices. Is God hearing us complain, or is He hearing us share our expectations?

> "...for of the abundance of the heart his mouth speaketh". **Luke 6:45** When we speak faith, it

makes our faith grow. But the opposite is true, speaking doubt also makes our doubt grow.

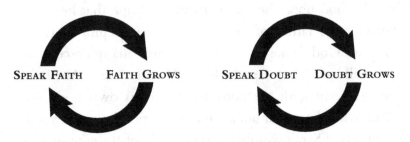

SPEAK FAITH   FAITH GROWS   SPEAK DOUBT   DOUBT GROWS

"A good man out of the good treasure of his heart bringeth forth that which is good; and an evil man out of the evil treasure of his heart bringeth forth that which is evil: for of the abundance of the heart his mouth speaketh."
Luke 6:45 (KJV)

COMPLAINING DESTROYS HOPE

66**D**on't complain as some of them did. The angel of death destroyed them" (1 Corinthians 10:10, GW). Our words can strengthen or weaken our hope. God changed Abram's name to Abraham, which translates to "Father of many." Every time he or someone said his name, it strengthened his hope—his expectation—in God's promise. Again, only Caleb and Joshua entered the Promised Land because they did not complain but believed—trusted in the Lord—that God wanted them to take the land (Numbers 14:28–35, AMP).

I believe Zacharias was made mute so he would not destroy the expectation of John the Baptist. In Luke 1:18–20 (KJV) said,

> And Zacharias said unto the angel, whereby shall I know this? For I am an old man, and my wife is well stricken in years. And the angel answering said unto him, I am Gabriel that stands in the presence of God; and am sent to speak unto thee and to shew thee these glad tidings. And, behold, thou shalt

MICHAEL BYRD, PH.D.

be dumb, and not able to speak, until the day
that these things shall be performed, because
thou believest not my words, which shall be
fulfilled in their season.

We, like Job, can trust God and say, "Though he slay
me, yet will I trust God!" (Job 13:15 KJV). Complaining
magnifies our problems. The more I complain about a
problem, the more it seems to overwhelm me. Moreover,
the harder it seems for me to fix. As I stated earlier, by
complaining and glorifying the problem, we indirectly
glorify the author of the problem. We talk about how bad
our problems are more than we talk about how great our
God is. By complaining, we give more glory to Satan than
we give to God!

Jesus said in Matthew 11:28 (KJV), "Come unto me, all
ye that labour and are heavy laden, and I will give you rest."
In other words, come to me all you who are totally stressed
out, and Jesus will give you restful peace.

Isaiah 26:3 (NKJV) tells us, "You will keep him in
perfect peace, Whose mind is stayed on You, Because he
trusts in You. In the original Hebrew, it reads, "You will
keep him in shalom shalom whose mind is stayed on you."
The first "shalom" is translated to the word "perfect." *Strong's
Hebrew Dictionary* defines "shalom" as "peace" or "perfect."
It continues with, "safe, well, happy, friendly; also, welfare,
health, prosperity, peace fare, favour, friend, great, (good)
health, (perfect, such as be at) peaceable, peaceably, prosperity,
prosperous, rest, safety, welfare, wholly." "Shalom" can also
be translated as "completeness" or "wholeness." So now we

see that God will keep us in perfect completeness if we keep our minds stayed on Him.

Satan is a master distracter. Satan distracts us from God. When we look at circumstances, we trust in what it looks like. We complain because we trust what it looks like. God wants us to trust and focus on Him. We focus on Him when we worship.

We find in Galatians 6:7 (KJV), "Be not deceived; God is not mocked: for whatsoever a man soweth, that shall he also reap." Whatever you sow, that will be what you reap! If you sow complaining, you will reap more to complain about. If you sow worship, you reap more to worship God for.

We need to speak (or prophesy) to our hopeless situations. The Bible says in Ezekiel 37:1–4 (KJV),

> The hand of the Lord was upon me, and carried me out in the spirit of the Lord, and set me down in the midst of the valley which [was] full of bones, And caused me to pass by them round about: and, behold, [there were] very many in the open valley; and, lo, [they were] very dry. And he said unto me, Son of man, can these bones live? And I answered, O Lord God, thou knowest. Again he said unto me, Prophesy upon these bones, and say unto them, O ye dry bones, hear the word of the Lord.

As a kid I heard a lot of sermons about the dry bones. But as a young adult, I learned what the dry bones represented. In Ezekiel 37:11 says, "Then He said unto me, Son of man, these bones are the whole house of Israel: behold, they say, Our bones are dried, and our hope is lost; we are cut off for our parts." We, too, need to prophesy or speak to our dry bones, our seemingly hopelessly despairing situations.

"'For I know the plans I have for you,' declares the Lord, "'plans to prosper you and not to harm you, plans to give you hope and a future'" (Jeremiah 29:11 NIV). In other words, God wants to prosper us and give us hope. God has great plans for us. However, God loves us and gives us free will to choose our ways or His way. God will not force His plans to prosper us on us. God loves us so much He gives us the choice to accept His will and plan—or not.

SELF-FULFILLING PROPHECY

The term "self-fulfilling prophecy" was coined by sociologist Robert Merton in 1948. He defined it as "a false definition of the situation evoking a new behavior which makes the originally false conception come true." I believe our lives are self-fulfilling prophecies. A person's belief and expectations create a situation that makes that belief come true. We have a need for security. Our security comes only from trusting God. As Psalm 20:7 (AMP) says, "Some trust in and boast of chariots and some of horses, but we will trust in and boast of the name of the Lord our God." In other words, in today's vernacular, some trust in power, and some trust in money. But I will trust in the Lord. Since we get what we believe, if you believe that God is your protector, which causes you to believe you live in a safe world, then you will. And if you believe that you live in an unsafe world, then you will as well.

Being a black man, I realize that there are people who hate and want to kill me just because of the color of my skin. But I choose to believe I live in a safe world because I stand on Psalm 91:10–11 (KJV): "There shall no evil befall thee(me), neither shall any plague come nigh thy (my) dwelling. For he God) shall give his angels charge over thee (me), to keep (protect) thee (me) in all thy (my) ways." David, the author of the above scripture, was a man of war. His enemies were always trying to kill him, but he said in Psalm 23:4 (KJV), "Yea, though I walk through the valley of the shadow of death, I will fear no evil: for thou art with me." I grew up in a tough inner-city neighborhood. I do not remember being bullied or picked on until middle school. I witnessed other kids my age being bullied and picked on in elementary school, but not me. In my adult life, I realized it was because of my huge, bodybuilding oldest brother. It was when he went into the military when I was in the sixth grade that I began being bullied and picked on. I realize now I have a stronger and more powerful big brother—Jesus. I encourage my reader to meditate and say aloud to yourself, "I am safe." "I am at peace." "God is with me." "God loves me."

I was told some stories about self-fulfilling prophecies. The first one is about a man who was accidentally locked in a refrigerated train car over the weekend. Expecting to freeze to death, he began to write on the walls. He said goodbye to his loved ones and expressed his regrets. The last thing he wrote was, "This may be the last thing I write." When they found his body after the weekend, they were surprised at his death. Not only did the refrigeration not work, but it had been taken out of the car. He fulfilled his prophecy. His belief and expectation created the situation that made his belief come true. He believed he was unsafe, which caused him to be unsafe. The Bible says, "We are saved by hope [our positive expectations]" (Romans 8:24 KJV). We are also destroyed by our lack of hope (negative expectation).

Working with students, I have seen how their lack of hope and holding on to negative expectations often led down a road to destruction.

The second is of survivors of a plane crash. The pilots were killed in the crash. The survivors did not know where they were or which direction to go to find help. They did find a map in a foreign language they didn't understand. For weeks they followed the mountains and rivers on the map to find civilization. When they did, everyone was surprised as the rescuers had given up on finding them. The rescuers wondered how they could have survived so long without help. They wondered why they didn't give up. The survivors said they would have given up weeks ago if they didn't have that map to lead them. The rescuers looked at the map and saw that it was not only not from their country but not even from the same continent. The survivors' faith in that wrong map gave them the hope to keep going. They were saved by hope.

I was eating lunch with two young men and was surprised to hear them talking about not, *if* they were going to prison, but *when* they go to prison and how they would deal with the challenges of prison life. They did not have jobs, and they believed they lived in an environment that was a one-way road to prison. Their only way of making money was what they called, "hitting a lick," or robbing someone weaker, or stealing. They had the mindset of laugh now, cry later. Their belief system was that life is short and unfair, so you have to take advantage of the weaknesses of others, even though they realized that bad decisions lead to pain later. I worked hard to change their stronghold on this thinking.

I believe there are thousands of young people with those

same hopeless belief systems outside my direct sphere of contact. It is my hope and prayer that this book will find them and show them how to make earth—their world—like heaven by destroying negative self-fulfilling prophecies.

THE BATTLE IS FOR OUR THOUGHTS AND EMOTIONS

If Satan can control our thoughts and emotions, he can control the direction of our lives. I am always saying, "If Satan can control how you think and feel, he can control your decisions and actions."

> For though we walk in the flesh, we do not war after the flesh: For the weapons of our warfare are not carnal, but mighty through God to the pulling down of strong holds; Casting down imaginations, and every high thing that exalteth itself against the knowledge of God, and bringing into captivity every thought to the obedience of Christ. (2 Corinthians 10:3–5 KJV)

I remember the homegoing celebration of my father. Right in the middle of praising God, my mind began to remember my father, and I began to miss him. I had to get my thoughts under control. I had to remember that I was not saying goodbye; I was saying, "I will see you later!" I know it is sometimes hard to think about godly things when we are battling in our minds, but that is why we should die to our selfish thoughts and emotions. I try to be like Paul in 1 Corinthians 15:31 (KJV), when he says, "I die daily." I'm reminded of 1 Thessalonians 4:13 (KJV): "But I would not have you to be ignorant, brethren, concerning them which are asleep, that ye sorrow not, even as others which have no hope." Furthermore, Jesus said in Matthew 10:38 (KJV), "And he that taketh not his cross, and followeth after me, is not worthy of me." If we are not willing to die to self our desires, we are not worthy of Him.

Jesus said in John 10:10 (KJV), "I am come that they might have life, and that they might have it more abundantly." Also, John 8:36 (KJV) states, "If the Son therefore shall make you free, ye shall be free indeed." We can choose to walk in that freedom, or we can allow Satan to control how we think and feel, and our decisions and actions.

As a former boxer, I learned that the fastest or stronger fighters don't always win. Speed can be timed for counterpunches, and strength can be smothered or avoided. We are the stronger, faster fighters, but Satan has studied us like a champion prizefighter, who learns the opponent's strengths and weaknesses to take advantage of us. We, too, should learn our opponent's strategies so that we can fight the way God wants us to fight. Our thoughts want to try to overcome worldly problems with worldly solutions, but the weapons of our warfare are not worldly. Rather, they are mighty spiritual thoughts that overpower negative thoughts. Two of the most powerful weapons we can use are love and forgiveness.

There were two camps of thought in winning the civil

rights battle. These two ways were the natural ways of retaliation and violence, and the spiritual way of nonviolence, love, and forgiveness. Those in the camp advocating violence believed that if someone hit you, you should hit the person back. If someone killed one of you, then you should kill one of them. If they used force to keep you out, then you should use force to make your way in.

Civil rights were won through the other camp, which advocated a spiritual approach of love, forgiveness, and many prayers! I believe that we would not have the civil rights we have today if the fight had been fought in the natural arena with guns and knives. In the battles in your life, are you fighting in the natural or spiritual realm? Are you using hate or love? Remember that love is stronger than hate.

Galatians 5:6 (KJV) tells us, "but faith which worketh by love." Love is God's operating system. Love has changed America from discrimination to a not free but freer country. I encourage readers to read *Deal with the Hurt, or the Hurt Will Deal with You,* a twelve-step process of forgiving past hurts.

Jesus wants to make earth like heaven. Satan wants to make earth like hell. We are in charge of what the world looks like. Death and life are in the power of the tongue. We Christians sometimes fight using Satan's weapons of speaking curses toward people. We dehumanize people by speaking badly about them. Historically, when America fought against people (Native Americans, the Chinese, and African Americans, to name a few), they dehumanized them to make it easier to hurt or kill them.

Satan is trying to create an environment of hate. What we say reinforces what we think and feel. Speaking hate makes your hate grow.

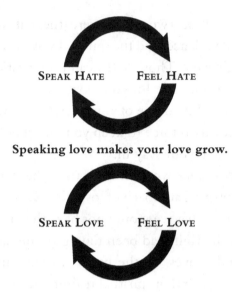

SPEAK HATE   FEEL HATE

Speaking love makes your love grow.

SPEAK LOVE   FEEL LOVE

As he loved cursing, so let it come unto him: as he delighted not in blessing, so let it be far from him. (Psalm 109:17 KJV)

He loved to curse others, so let those bad things happen to him. He never blessed others, so don't let good things happen to him. (Psalm 109:17 ERV)

We get to choose, according to Deuteronomy 30:19 (KJV). "I call heaven and earth to record this day against you, that I have set before you life and death, blessing and cursing: therefore choose life that both thou and thy seed may live."

When we choose to bless others, we are choosing life. Likewise, when we choose to curse others, we are choosing death. We walk by faith, not by sight. In other words, we practice faith no matter what it looks or feels like. We pull down strongholds by controlling thought patterns that lead to what we say. We cast down imaginations and every high thing that exalts itself against the knowledge of God by what we say.

Life and death, blessing and cursing are in our control. The battle is for our thoughts and emotions. One of the fruits of the spirit is self-control. The more we control our thoughts and emotions, the more we control our futures. The less we control our thoughts and emotions, the less we control our futures. For example, the more you can control your anger, the more you can control your future; the less you can control your anger, the less you can control your future. Who do you want to be in control of your life ... you or Satan?

> I press toward the goal for the prize of the upward call of God in Christ Jesus. (Philippians 3:14 NKJV)

When I counsel young people about building self-esteem, I tell them one of the best ways to build self-esteem and feel good about themselves is to achieve goals. I tell them that successful people think differently than unsuccessful people. If you have set and reached most of your goals, it creates a belief system that you can reach future goals—have hope and positive expectations. But if you have not set and reached many goals, it creates a belief system that you can't reach your goals—low or no expectations.

In my experience, students who have been labeled as unmotivated, in reality are students who do not believe they have the ability to achieve academically. When they achieve an academic goal, they become more focused and more determined to reach future goals. If they never reach a goal, their belief system becomes based on failure. When these students finally reach a goal, they have an expectation of setting and reaching future goals.

> Now the God of hope fill you with all joy and peace in believing that ye may abound in hope through the power of the Holy Ghost. (Romans 15:13 KJV)

Since God is the God of positive expectations, He wants you to have positive expectations. We tend to go toward what we focus on. While I was in college, I learned how to ride a motorcycle. Years later, a friend got a new motorcycle. It had been a few years since I'd driven one, but I thought, *I remember how to ride. I'll just go slow.* I was turning a corner slowly, and as I looked to the side, I fell off the bike in the direction I was looking. I didn't learn from that. Years later I was on a dirt bike on a rocky trail going fast when turning a corner. When I began to look to where I didn't want to go, I fell again. This time it was painful enough for me to learn to always look to where I wanted to go, and never look to where I didn't want to go.

Besides exhibiting this tendency in the natural world, we also tend to go in the spiritual direction in which we focus our attention. In short, our lives gravitate to what we focus on. Satan wants us to focus on our failures. Life is like the game of baseball. If your batting average is 300 or better, you are at the top of your game since most people are batting well below 300. But if you are batting 300 it means that seven hundred times, or 70 percent of the time that you come to bat, you get an out. The better batters focus on their successes, not their failures. They focus on their hits, not on their misses. The more they focus on their hits, the better their chances of making a hit. The more they focus on their misses, the greater their likelihood of missing. So, too, in all life's situations, the more we focus on the good things in life, the better the chances of good things happening. The more we focus on the bad things in life, the better the chances of bad things happening.

Satan tries to get us to keep focusing on our mistakes. I remember as a kid being jumped, but no one has beaten me up for as long as I have beaten up myself. Satan can't hold anyone back, but he tries to get us to hold ourselves back by having us focus on our mistakes. If Satan can control our thoughts and emotions, he can control our futures. We should say, like Paul in Philippians 3:13 (KJV), "forgetting those things which are behind, and reaching forth unto those things which are before." The enemy wants you to think the worse about yourself and others. God wants us to "be not conformed to this world: but be ye transformed by the renewing of your mind, that ye may prove what is that good, and acceptable, and perfect, will of God" (Romans 12:2 KJV).

When we talk and think about negative things, we create negative strongholds of thinking. Every thought creates a neuropathway in the brain. The more we think a thought, positive or negative, the stronger the neuropathway gets. Imagine you are going through a thick jungle on a small trail. The more you travel the trail, the easier it gets and the more frightening it is to get off the trail. It is like drawing a straight line against the grain on a piece of wood. Your pen will zigzag because of the wood's grain. But once we make a groove in the wood, we tend to stay in the groove. The same goes for our thinking. The longer our thinking stays in the groove, the harder it becomes to get out of that groove. The more we think negative, the harder it is to get out of that groove of negative thinking. The deeper the groove gets, the harder it is to control the thoughts, and the thoughts control more and more of the person's life. We have to control our thoughts or our thoughts will control us! The Bible tells us in Romans 8:6 (NIV), "The mind governed by the flesh is death, but the mind governed by the Spirit is life and peace." When we repeatedly fail to reach our goals, we tend to believe we can't reach any goals, so we don't try very hard. This thinking sets us up for failure, reinforcing the belief that we couldn't do it in the first place. Reinforcing negative thoughts is conforming to this world. We are commanded to think on these things; "whatsoever things are true, whatsoever things are honest, whatsoever things are just, whatsoever things are pure, whatsoever things are lovely, whatsoever things are of good report; if there be any virtue, and if there be any praise, think on these things" (Philippians 4:8 KJV).

When we think about the things we did right and not what we did wrong, we are transforming our minds to Christ. I encourage my students to set big goals, or long-term goals. I admonish them that no goal is too big if they have enough short-term goals to reach for each long-term goal. I ask them to have seven or more short-term goals on the path to each long-term goal, and seven or more strategies to reach each short-term goal. You can write your goals in this book, but write and celebrate each goal achieved in a place where you can see them and acknowledge them; for example, have a sheet for short-term goals and another for long-term goals. Or write the following chart out on a sheet of paper. Focusing on your achievements creates a belief that you can achieve things. But focusing on failures creates a belief that you will fail at things. Focusing on your wins creates a belief system, as does focusing on losses. Winners remember and focus on their wins. Losers remember and focus on their losses.

Focus on goals achieved. Highly motivated people believe that they can succeed at things in life. And highly unmotivated people believe that they can't succeed at things in life. Focusing on your accomplishments and goals reached creates a belief system for success, creating an expectation of success. Focusing on your failures and goals not reached creates a belief system of failure, creating an expectation of failure. God wants to create a belief system that gives you, "thoughts of peace, and not of evil, to give you an expected end [hope]" (Jeremiah 29:11 KJV).

Short-Term Goals	Strategies to Reach Short-Term Goals: Steps to Achieve This Goal		Goal Date	Evaluation: Did I Achieve the Goals?
	1. 2. 3. 4.	5. 6. 7.		
	1. 2. 3. 4.	5. 6. 7.		
	1. 2. 3. 4.	5. 6. 7.		
	1. 2. 3. 4.	5. 6. 7.		
	1. 2. 3. 4.	5. 6. 7.		

Long-Term Goals	Long-Term Goals: How Can I Achieve the Goals?		Goal Date	Evaluation: Did I Achieve the Goals?
	1. 2. 3. 4.	5. 6. 7.		
	1. 2. 3. 4.	5. 6. 7.		
	1. 2. 3. 4.	5. 6. 7.		
	1. 2. 3. 4.	5. 6. 7.		
	1. 2. 3. 4.	5. 6. 7.		

WHY AM I DEPRESSED?

King David asked himself that question in Psalm 42:5 (CEB): "Why, I ask myself, are you so depressed? Why are you so upset inside? Hope in God! Because I will again give him thanks, my saving presence and my God."

Why am I allowing thoughts of depression to dominate my thinking and feelings? Again, I believe our thoughts and feelings of hope can overcome our feelings of depression. Or we can allow our feelings of depression to overcome our feelings of hope. King David answered that question with, "Hope in God!" I hope in God's promises or have positive expectations in God.

Romans 8:28 (KJV) says, "And we know that all things work together for good to them that love God, to them who are the called according to his purpose." Although it looks hopeless, we expect things to work out for the good for us.

Romans 8:37 (KJV) says, "Nay, in all these things we are more than conquerors through him that loved us." Although it looks like we will be destroyed, we are more than conquerors because God loves us. We must remind ourselves of 2 Corinthians 4:17–18 (KJV):

> For our light affliction, which is but for a moment, worketh for us a far more exceeding and eternal weight of glory; While we look not at the things which are seen, but at the things which are not seen: for the things which are seen are temporal; but the things which are not seen are eternal.

I have learned that the more I focus on my small afflictions, the bigger they seem. Satan wants us to focus on our afflictions, but God wants us to focus on the benefits—glory—of overcoming the affliction. We look not at the things that are seen—afflictions—but at the things that are not seen—our positive expectations.

> Why am I discouraged? Why is my heart so sad? I will put my hope in God! I will praise him again—my Savior and my God. (Psalm 42:5 NLT)

When I first began counseling students in school, I began to get depressed. This would happen because I would have to send the child back home after contacting child protection services about the danger of abuse. I would get depressed until I learned to trust God in each situation.

I believe the answer to the question why am I depressed is to have hope and trust in the Lord. We can allow our hope to overpower our depression or we can allow our depression to overpower our hope (Psalm 31:24 GW): "Be strong, all who wait with hope for the Lord, and let your heart be courageous." We can agree with the Bible and wait with hope for the Lord.

I had a former student describe his depression as a feeling of hopelessness. Once he found hope, he was no longer depressed.

OVERCOME DEPRESSION THROUGH WORSHIP

I believe we were created to praise and worship God. I also believe we strengthen our relationships with God through praise and worship. Through praise and worship we express our love for God. Many people experience sadness because they lack a relationship with God. Paul says the following in Romans 1:21 (KJV): "Because of that, when they knew God, they glorified him not as God, neither were thankful; but became vain in their imaginations, and their foolish *heart was darkened*" (emphasis added). Other versions word the italicized phrase as, "hearts were filled with darkness" (EXB) and "plunged into darkness" (GW).

Can this darkness be depression? Could it be due to growing unthankfulness and lack of worship of God? Paul seems to imply we should worship in times of trouble. Paul also implies that Abraham did as well in Romans 4:19–20 (KJV):

> And being not weak in faith, he considered
> not his own body now dead, when he was

about an hundred years old, neither yet the
deadness of Sara's womb: He staggered not at
the promise of God through unbelief; but was
strong in faith, giving glory to God.

King David says in Psalm 42:5 (KJV), "Why art thou
cast down, O my soul? and why art thou disquieted in me?
hope thou in God: for I shall yet praise him for the help of
his countenance." Likewise, Job, after learning he had lost
everything in Job 1:20 (KJV), says, "Then Job arose, and
rent his mantle, and shaved his head, and fell down upon the
ground, and worshipped." Paul, David, Job, and Abraham
were four of the great men of faith who worshipped during
times of trouble.

Historically, black people would go to church to shout
and praise God. People in the early black church lived in a
hostile world where they had to trust God. The more they
worshipped, the more they trusted God, and the more they
trusted God, the more they worshiped. They hoped, even
though change seemed impossible. We, too, should worship
God in our seemingly impossible situations. "And we know
that all things work together for good to them that love God,
to them who are called according to his purpose" (Romans
8:28 KJV). When we know that all things are working for
our good, we will praise and worship God. If we don't trust
that things will work out, we will complain. "Worship God
if you want the best; worship opens doors to all his goodness"
(Psalm 34:9 MSG). I believe we should worship God if we
expect the best. I expect God to keep His promises. "God
is not a man that he should lie" (Numbers 23:19 KJV). We

can worship God because we trust Him and know that all things are going to work out for our good.

> We continue to shout our praise even when we're hemmed in with troubles because we know how troubles can develop passionate patience in us, and how that patience, in turn, forges the tempered steel of virtue, keeping us alert for whatever God will do next. In alert expectancy such as this, we're never left feeling shortchanged. Quite the contrary. We can't round up enough containers to hold everything God generously pours into our lives through the Holy Spirit! (Romans 5:4–5 MSG) We should; offer the sacrifice of praise to God continually, that is, the fruit of *our* lips giving thanks to his name. **Hebrews 13:15 (KJV)**

In Pentecostal churches, dancing is believed to be dancing on the devil's head. Also, the clapping of hands in worship drives the devils away. Earlier I talked about boxers learning the weaknesses of their opponents so that they may win. I believe true worship can drive out the enemy and his attack of depression and anxiety. Again, Psalm 34:9 (MSG): "Worship God if you want the best; worship opens doors to all his goodness." Thank God for the positive expectations. Thank God for it before you receive it! Rejoice with the positive expectation of the good things you want.

When I'm feeling down, I meditate and sing the children's

hymn, "Jesus Loves Me, This I Know" by Susan Bogert Warner and Anna Bartlett Warner in 1859.

Jesus loves me—this I know, For the Bible tells me so; Little ones to him belong—They are weak, but he is strong. Yes, Jesus loves me! Yes, Jesus loves me! Yes, Jesus loves me! For the bible tells me so! Jesus loves me when I'm good! When I do the things I should! And Jesus loves me when I'm bad! Although it makes Him very sad! Yes, Jesus loves me.

I focus on the fact that Jesus loves me and that fills me with joy! The songs we sing to ourselves reinforce our feelings. I encourage students to stop listening to depressing music or music that talks about suicide.

JOY

J oy comes from trusting in God. Trust in God leads to hope. Romans 15:13 (KJV) says, "Now the God of hope fill you with all joy and peace in believing, that ye may abound in hope, through the power of the Holy Ghost." The Greek word for "believing" can be translated as "entrust." Also, Psalm 5:11 (KJV) states, "But let all those that put their trust in thee rejoice: let them ever shout for joy, because thou defendest them: let them also that love thy name be joyful in thee." James 1:2–4 (AMP) tells us, "Consider it nothing but joy, my brothers and sisters, whenever you fall into various trials. Be assured that the testing of your faith [through experience] produces endurance [leading to spiritual maturity, and inner peace]. And let endurance have its perfect result and do a thorough work, so that you may be perfect and completely developed [in your faith], lacking in nothing."

Again, I believe the challenges in life come to help us grow in our trust or faith in God. We should count it all joy when facing difficulties because they help us mature and learn to trust in God. Jesus said, "These things have I spoken unto you, that my joy might remain in you, and that your joy might be full" (John 15:11 KJV). We can choose to receive God's joy.

Deuteronomy talks about the blessings for keeping God's commandments and the cursing for not keeping them. God said, "Because thou servest not the Lord thy God with joyfulness, and with gladness of heart, for the abundance of all things" (Deuteronomy 28:47 KJV). We, like the children of Israel in the wilderness, focus on the things we didn't have and are not thankful (joyful) for what God has given us!

I know God has saved me and is conforming me to His kingdom. I should always serve Him with joy and gladness, but sometimes I lose sight of what He has done in my life. I look at all the circumstances in life and sometimes walk by sight, not by faith. I have to get back into God's presence in worship. "In thy presence is fullness of joy" (Psalm 16:11 KJV).

I encourage you to read *Attitude of Gratitude True Worship* to help you rejoice in hope. When we focus on the things we are thankful for, we find joy.

> And now shall mine head be lifted up above mine enemies round about me: therefore will I offer in his tabernacle sacrifices of joy; I will sing, yea, I will sing praises unto the Lord. (Psalm 27:6 KJV)

The second fruit of the fruits of the Spirit is joy according to Galatians 5:22 (KJV), which says: "But the fruit of the Spirit is love, joy, peace, long suffering, gentleness, goodness, faith." We learn in Psalm 5:11 (AMP) to "let all those who take refuge and put their trust in You rejoice; let them ever sing and shout for joy, because You make a covering over them and defend them; let those also who love Your name be joyful in You and be in high spirits." God's cover protects you when you praise Him. When we feel hopeless, we should give God a sacrifice of joy. "I will sing, yea, I will sing praises unto the Lord" (Psalm 27:6 KJV). Why? Because the scripture says, "Nehemiah said, "Go and enjoy the good food and sweet drinks. Give some food and drinks to those who didn't prepare any food. Today is a special day to our Lord. Don't be sad, because the joy of the Lord will make you strong." (Nehemiah 8:10 ERV). Sadness causes weakness. But joy strengthens us! God wants to strengthen us. But Satan wants to weaken us.

I was told by my childhood pastor Elder Huland Williams that happiness comes from circumstances. But Joy is a choice. You can choose to be joyful or not. The only power Satan has over us is the power we give him. Satan tries to keep us in negative emotions. Satan knows if he can control negative emotions in our lives, he can control our decisions. So, I say: "Rejoice in the Lord always. I will say it again: Rejoice!" (Romans 4:4 NIV)

WHEN HOPE IS CRUSHED, THE HEART IS CRUSHED

Proverbs 13:12 (GNT) tells us, "When hope is crushed, the heart is crushed, but a wish come true fills you with joy." "Above all else, guard your heart, for everything you do flows from it" (Proverbs 4:23 NIV).

The enemy has awakened me in the middle of the night with overpowering feelings and thoughts of hopelessness. I immediately remind myself to say, "I trust you, Lord!" Jesus said in Luke 6:45 (KJV) that "a good man out of the good treasure of his heart bringeth forth that which is good, and an evil man out of the evil treasure of his heart bringeth forth that which is evil: for of the abundance of the heart the mouth speaketh."

If we have an abundance of doubt, we are likely to speak doubt. But if we have an abundance of faith and trust in God, we will be more likely to speak faith and trust in God. If I am walking and accidentally stub my toe and cursing comes out of my mouth, the pain in my toe did not put the cursing in my mouth; it just revealed what was in my heart. The question comes up, How do we build faith and trust in

God in our hearts? Romans 10:17 (KJV) tells us, "So then, faith cometh by hearing and hearing by the word of God." "The point is, before you trust, you have to listen. But unless Christ's Word is preached, there's nothing to listen to" (Romans 10:17 MSG).

The person we listen to more than anyone is ourselves. "Speaking to yourselves in psalms and hymns and spiritual songs, singing and making melody in your heart to the Lord; Giving thanks always for all things unto God and the Father in the name of our Lord Jesus Christ" (Ephesians 5:19–20 KJV). Our enemy wants to crush our hope, thereby crushing our confidence and faith in God. "Now faith is confidence in what we hope for and assurance about what we do not see" (Hebrews 11:1 NIV). "O Israel, hope in the Lord; for with the Lord there is loving kindness, And with Him is abundant redemption" (Psalm 130:7 NASB). "You will be secure, because there is hope; you will look about you and take your rest in safety" (Job 11:18 NIV).

We can believe we live in a safe world. We can say like David, a man of war, says in Psalm 91:7 (KJV) that "a thousand shall fall at thy side, and ten thousand at thy right hand; but it shall not come nigh thee." Even in our world of illness—like COVID-19—wars, and terrorism, we, too, should say, "a thousand shall fall at my side and ten thousand at my right hand; but it shall not come nigh me!" We keep our hopes and hearts from being crushed by singing and speaking God's Word.

THE SCRIPTURES GIVE US HOPE

Romans 15:4 (ERV) tells us, "Everything that was written in the past was written to teach us. Those things were written so that we could have hope. That hope comes from the patience and encouragement that the Scriptures give us." First Corinthians 10:11 (KJV) says, "Now all these things happened unto them for examples: and they are written for our admonition, upon whom the ends of the world are come." We try to fight the enemy without admonitions.

When I am feeling hopeless, I quote Isaiah 51:10 (MSG): "Didn't you once dry up the sea, the powerful waters of the deep, and then make the bottom of the ocean a road for the redeemed to walk across?" I imagine seeing myself trapped by a large enemy rushing to attack me from behind, and there is only a great river in front of me. And then the river opening for me. I quote Psalm 91:1–16 (KJV):

> He that dwelleth in the secret place of the most High shall abide under the shadow of the Almighty. I will say of the Lord, He is my refuge and my fortress; my God; in him

will I trust. Surely he shall deliver thee from the snare of the fowler, and from the noisome pestilence. He shall cover thee with his feathers, and under his wings shalt thou trust; his truth shall be thy shield and buckler. Thou shalt not be afraid for the terror by night; nor for the arrow that flieth by day; nor for the pestilence that walketh in darkness; nor for the destruction that wasteth at noonday. A thousand shall fall at thy side, and ten thousand at thy right hand; but it shall not come nigh thee. Only with thine eyes shalt thou behold and see the reward of the wicked. Because thou hast made the Lord, which is my refuge, even the most High, thy habitation; There shall no evil befall thee [me], neither shall any plague come nigh thy dwelling. For he shall give his angels charge over thee, to keep thee in all thy ways. They shall bear thee up in their hands, lest thou dash thy foot against a stone. Thou shalt tread upon the lion and adder: the young lion and the dragon shalt thou trample under feet. Because he hath set his love upon me, therefore will I deliver him: I will set him on high, because he hath known my name. He shall call upon me, and I will answer him: I will be with him in trouble; I will deliver him, and honour him. With long life will I satisfy him, and shew him my salvation.

I also quote Deuteronomy 28:8 (AMP), which says: "The Lord will command the blessing upon you in your storehouses and in all that you undertake, and He will bless you in the land which the Lord your God gives you." And Isaiah 53:5 (AMP) says, "But He was wounded for our transgressions, He was crushed for our wickedness [our sin, our injustice, our wrongdoing]; The punishment [required] for our well-being fell on Him, And by His stripes [wounds] we are healed." Just as Jesus used the scriptures to fight Satan, I also use the scripture to overcome Satan's attacks.

BE STRONG AND OF GOOD COURAGE

"Be strong and of good courage" is the theme and word spoken to the children of Israel going into the Promised Land. In the Old Testament (KJV) it says to be of good courage sixteen times. It does take courage to overtake and maintain God's promises.

Isaiah 41:10 (AMP) tells us, "Fear not [there is nothing to fear], for I am with you; do not look around you in terror and be dismayed, for I am your God. I will strengthen and harden you to difficulties, yes, I will help you; yes, I will hold you up and retain you with my [victorious] right hand of rightness and justice."

When we trust God, we have nothing to fear. We walk by faith; in other words, we don't look around looking at the circumstances. We look to the God of hope for He is with us. "And we know that all things work together for good to them that love God, to them who are called according to his purpose" (Romans 8:28 KJV). When we know that all things are working for our good, we will praise God. But when we don't know that all things are working for our good, we will complain.

As mentioned earlier, many people believe they live in an unsafe world. This is why I believe we have so many murders in places like Chicago. Psalm 119:165 (KJV) reads, "Great peace have they which love thy law: and nothing shall offend them." The word "offend" is mik-shole in Strong's Hebrew Dictionary, which also means to cause to stumble or fall. 1 John 2:10 He that loveth his brother abideth in the light, and there is none occasion of stumbling in him. In Strong's Greek Dictionary the word for stumbling is skan'-dal-on; which also means to offend. Matthew 18:6 But whoso shall offend one of these little ones which believe in me, it were better for him that a millstone were hanged about his neck, and that he were drowned in the depth of the sea. In Strong's Greek Dictionary the word for offend skan-dal-id'-zo; which also means to cause to stumble. Satan wants us to be offended and to cause us to offend others as to get us out of walking in love (practicing love). Black people were offended by the police killing unarmed blacks during protests some people looted stores which cause others to be offended. People got offended when Donald Trump lost and stormed the Nation's capital. I have learned the more we walk or practice love, the harder it is to offend us or cause us to fall. But I have found the opposite is true as well. The less we walk or practice love, the easier it is to get offended or to stumble and get angry than hurt people. Hurting people hurt people creating a belief that they are unsafe. When someone believes he or she is unsafe, the person may believe his or her life has little value. And because one's life doesn't have value, others' lives don't have value. This often creates a cycle of hurt and counter-hurt and offends and counter-offends. In quantum physics, every thought emits a frequency toward the universe, and that frequency returns toward the source of origin. If you have negative thoughts of discouragement, sadness, anger, and fear, all of that turns toward you. In other words, we create a safe or hostile world. Our Creator created us in His image and likeness to create as well.

Paul said in Galatians 6:7 (KJV), "Be not deceived; God is not mocked: for whatsoever a man soweth, that shall he also reap." If we sow fear, we will reap more to fear. If we believe we live in a hostile and unsafe world, we will be fearful.

One of the biggest things I have found that determines whether one becomes successful or not is courage. I have seen many young people too afraid to try even though they had talent and the intelligence enough to become successful. I have also seen young people who were not as smart and talented but had the courage to try to become successful. I have realized that there are two primary routes to courage: (1) experiences and (2) encouragement. There is a saying, "The best teacher is experience!"

As a young kid, we spent our summers at the neighborhood swimming pool. Once we showed the lifeguard that we could swim across the width of the swimming pool, we were allowed in the deep end of the pool. The pool had two diving boards, a high dive and a low dive. My friends and I began jumping off the low diving board. We learned to dive, and some of us learned to flip off the low diving board. But a few of my friends began to jump from the high diving board. Even some of my more timid friends began to jump from the high dive. I climbed up several times without jumping off. The rule was you could only climb up the ladder, not down it. But after I stayed on the board for so long, the lifeguard would say, "Byrd come down." My friends made fun of me and talked about me badly for not jumping. They would say, "Byrd, how can you be a bird and be afraid of heights?" I would climb up, walk to the end of the board, look down, and say to myself, "No way! I can't do it!" But my friends eventually stopped making fun of me and started to encourage me, saying, "You can do it!" Once I did jump off the high diving board, I began to cut in line to jump off the high dive!

The best teacher is experience because experience develops confidence. Once I jumped, it gave me the confidence to keep jumping. Experience! Because of our experiences, we gain confidence. I believe David gained the courage to face a bear because he experienced overcoming the lion. In addition, he had the courage to face the giant because he had the experiences of facing the lion and bear. When we don't get experience, we often don't do things because of a lack of confidence (experience). Some people don't apply for jobs because they believe they are not qualified. Some don't go to college because they don't think they can finish. But the fact is, they don't have confidence and experience; confidence is what we need to go forward. Experiences that we have in trusting in God develop confidence and trust in God. I believe God wants us all to have an unshakable trust in Him.

The second-best teacher is encouragement. We live in a world where people know right from wrong but don't always have the courage to do the right thing. In 1 Corinthians 10:9 (KJV), Paul compares Christians to the Israelites in the desert trying to go to the Promised Land. The biggest theme the leaders said to the Israelites was, "Be of good courage!" It would take courage to take and maintain the Promised Land. I believe the same is true for Christians today. Christians today are not walking into God's promises (or Promised Land). I believe we get courage from encouragement! And as I said earlier, I also believe the person we listen to more than any other is ourselves. I believe we have to do as David did in 1 Samuel 30:6 (KJV) in one of his most difficult times before he became king. We, too, have to encourage ourselves. Courage is not the lack of fear but the overcoming of fear. We have to overcome our fears, or our fears will overcome us! We gain the courage to overcome our fears by encouraging ourselves.

We also become discouraged—or have a lack of courage—when people discourage us. It is common to put down or make fun of others. I believe we have so many shootings in America because dehumanization makes it easier to kill. Merriam-Webster.com defines dehumanize as: (a) "to subject (someone, such as a prisoner) to conditions or treatment that are inhumane or degrading," and b) "to address or portray (someone) in a way that obscures or demeans that person's humanity or individuality." I define it to be when people speak about or treat people badly to make them feel less than human. I believe if you treat people with respect, you get respect back. You treat them like animals by strip-searching them, you dehumanize them; you dehumanize yourself. You can't put down someone without putting down yourself. If I call someone stupid to make it seem like I am better, I am reinforcing, on the subconscious level, the hurt that I felt when someone called me that. Hurting people hurts people. People put others down to try to make themselves think they are better than the person they are putting down.

An example of this was June 7, 1998, in Jasper, Texas, when Shawn Berry, Lawrence Brewer, and John King dragged James Byrd Jr. for three miles behind a pickup. This racial crime was reported around the world. People would ask me how I felt about the murder. I told them murders are performed to dehumanize or put someone down. The more you put someone down to feel better about yourself, the more you have to put someone down to feel better about yourself. Eventually, you must hurt someone to feel better about yourself. If you dehumanize someone long enough, you will make it easier to kill them. Historically, whenever American soldiers were taught to fight a battle, they were also taught to dehumanize the enemy to make it easier to kill them.

I believe we can cultivate an environment of courage by encouraging one another, thus fulfilling Jesus's prayer, "God's kingdom come, God's will be done on earth as it is in Heaven!"

Satan is trying to make earth like hell by having people cursing and dehumanizing others. We can choose to dehumanize people or to empower people. Jewish people are empowered and encouraged to gain wealth by the Priestly Prayer. But for many inner-city children, the first word they understand and articulate is "No!" No, don't this or that. Young children say no so often because they hear it so often. This creates a limitation mindset and a self-fulfilling prophecy that the children begin to live out in their lives. "I can't do anything good, so I'll do bad." This also creates a belief that the world is unsafe. It is hard to go forward in life looking backward or looking over your shoulder. The fear of living in an unsafe world keeps us focused on the here and now and not make plans for the future. I'm always telling kids, "Going through life without a plan is a hard life! If we believe we live in an unsafe world, we will not trust the world." "When we trust God, and we know that all things work together for good to them that love God, to them who are called according to his purpose (Romans 8:28 KJV). We grow to believe that we live in a safe world. When we trust God, we have confidence when in trouble. But when we don't trust God, we have fear when in trouble. I want my readers to have so much trust in God that they will say like David in Psalm 27:3 (KJV), "Though an host should encamp against me, my heart shall not fear: though war should rise against me, in this will I be confident." We, too, can gain confidence by trusting God. The more we trust God, the more He entrusts us, creating a growing cycle of maturely trusting relationships that, in turn, builds God's kingdom on earth as it is in heaven! Courage is not the lack of fear but the overcoming of fear.

FEAR

I was told that fear is the enemy of faith. I believe fear is the opposite of hope. Fear is negative expectations. Hope is positive expectations. Fear is both what we think and how we feel. Hope is also what we think and how we feel. An acronym for fear is:

> *F*alse
> *E*vidence
> *A*ppearing
> *R*eal

We need courage because our enemy attacks with FEAR.

Hebrews 11:1 (KJV) tells us, "Now faith is the substance of things hoped for, the evidence of things not seen." The word substance in Strong's Hebrew Dictionary hoop-os'-tas-is from a compound word (hupo) and (histemi); hupo: of, by, or with. Histemi: stand set established stand firm or sit or standstill. **Now faith is standing by that which we hoped for.** An example is the Freedom riders. Which stood and sat for freedom during the Civil Rights Movement. They stood by their faith. They faced their fears.

Romans 10:1 (KJV) says, "So then faith cometh by

hearing, and hearing by the word of God." We need to feed on the Word of God to strengthen our faith.

According to Proverbs 29:25 (KJV), "The fear of man bringeth a snare: but whoso putteth his trust in the Lord shall be safe." A good example is the boyfriend who is so afraid his girlfriend will leave him for someone else that his controlling, paranoid behavior causes her to do just that.

Job 3:25 (KJV) tells us, "For the thing which I greatly feared is come upon me and that which I was afraid of is come." Jesus and a father were going to heal the father's daughter when they heard a discouraging word.

Luke 8:49–50 (KJV) reads, "While he yet spake, there cometh one from the ruler of the synagogue's house, saying to him, Thy daughter is dead; trouble not the Master. But when Jesus heard it, he answered him, saying, Fear not: believe only, and she shall be made whole."

When Satan goes fishing, he throws out the bait on a hook (of false evidence appearing real). If we bite on the bait, he pulls us in. One of the biggest baits Satan uses is fear. Jesus is saying to you, "Fear not, only believe" (Mark 5:36 KJV).

According to Hebrews 10:23 (AMP), we have to confess and acknowledge our hope without wavering to overcome our fears. The scripture says, "So let us seize and hold fast and retain without wavering the hope we cherish and confess and our acknowledgment of it, for He Who promised is reliable (sure) and faithful to His word."

PRAYING IN THE SPIRIT

We pray God's will when we pray in the Spirit. "The Spirit helps us in our weakness. We do not know what we ought to pray for, but the Spirit intercedes for us through wordless groans. And he who searches our hearts knows the mind of the Spirit, because the Spirit intercedes for God's people in accordance with the will of God" (Romans 8:26–27 KJV). We also put on the full armor of God when we, "pray in the Spirit on all occasions with all kinds of prayers and requests" (Ephesians 6:13–18 KJV). With this in mind, be alert and always keep on praying for all the Lord's people. We fight spiritually when we pray in the spirit. This is how we fight the good fight of faith. Romans 8:26–27 (NIV) says, "In the same way, the Spirit helps us in our weaknesses. We do not know what we ought to pray for, but the Spirit himself intercedes for us through wordless groans. And he who searches our hearts knows the mind of the Spirit, because the Spirit intercedes for God's people in accordance with the will of God."

We don't know what to say in prayer. Ephesians 6:13–18 (NIV) tells us to "pray in the Spirit on all occasions with all kinds of prayers and requests." We build up and empower ourselves by praying in the Spirit. First Corinthians 14:4 (KJV) says that, "He that speaketh in an unknown tongue edifieth [build-up] himself; but he that prophesieth edifieth [build-up] the church." First Corinthians 14:4 (AMP) reads, "He who speaks in a [strange] tongue edifies and improves himself." We strengthen and improve ourselves by praying in the Spirit.

When we surrender our uncontrollable tongues to the Holy Spirit, we gain control over our whole bodies. James 3:8 (KJV) warns, "But the tongue can no man tame; it is an unruly evil, full of deadly poison." James 3:2 (KJV) advises, "For in many things we offend all. If any man offend not in word, the same is a perfect man, and able also to bridle the whole body."

PRAY WITHOUT CEASING

To pray without ceasing you must have hope. Jesus's disciples asked Him to teach them how to pray. After Jesus taught them the Lord's Prayer, He gave them an example.

And he said unto them, Which of you shall have a friend, and shall go unto him at midnight, and say unto him, Friend, lend me three loaves; For a friend of mine in his journey is come to me, and I have nothing to set before him? And he from within shall answer and say, Trouble me not: the door is now shut, and my children are with me in bed; I cannot rise and give thee. I say unto you, though he will not rise and give him, because he is his friend, yet because of his importunity he will rise and give him as many as he needeth. And I say unto you, Ask, and it shall be given you; seek, and ye shall find; knock, and it shall be opened unto you. For everyone that asketh, receiveth; and he that

seeketh, findeth; and to him that knocketh, it
shall be opened. (Luke 11:5–10 KJV)

The friend did not give him the bread because he was
a friend but because he asked without ceasing. I was told
that the Greek, words "ask," "seek," and "knock" are in the
continual tense. He who continues to ask or continues to
seek or continues to knock will receive.

Luke 11:5–10 (AMP) reads,

> Then He said to them, "Suppose one of you
> has a friend, and goes to him at midnight and
> says, 'Friend, lend me three loaves [of bread];
> for a friend of mine who is on a journey has
> just come to visit me, and I have nothing
> to serve him'; and from inside he answers,
> 'Do not bother me; the door has already
> been shut and my children and I are in bed;
> I cannot get up and give you anything.' I tell
> you, even though he will not get up and give
> him anything just because he is his friend,
> yet because of his persistence and boldness he
> will get up and give him whatever he needs.
> 'So I say to you, ask and keep on asking, and
> it will be given to you; seek and keep on
> seeking, and you will find; knock and keep
> on knocking, and the door will be opened
> to you. For everyone who keeps on asking
> [persistently], receives; and he who keeps on
> seeking [persistently], finds; and to him who

keeps on knocking [persistently], the door will be opened.'"

In other words, we must be persistent in prayer. We read in Luke 18:1–7 (KJV),

> And he spake a parable unto them to this end, that men ought always to pray, and not to faint; Saying, There was in a city a judge, which feared not God, neither regarded man: And there was a widow in that city; and she came unto him, saying, Avenge me of mine adversary. And he would not for a while: but afterward, he said within himself, Though I fear not God, nor regard man; Yet because this widow troubleth me, I will avenge her, lest by her continual coming she weary me. And the Lord said, Hear what the unjust judge saith. And shall not God avenge his own elect, which cry day and night unto him, though he bears long with them?

In this case, the widow reminded the judge of his duty. We, too, can remind God of His promises with an expectation to receive. I encourage you to read *Speaking God's Promises Changing Your World*. "Wherefore take unto you the whole armour of God, that ye may be able to withstand in the evil day, and having done all, to stand. Stand therefore" (Ephesians 6:13 KJV). We should be resilient in our prayers. Never give up because we win when we don't give in!

BLESSING OR CURSING

Earlier I referenced Deuteronomy 28 when talking about blessings. You receive blessings if you follow the commandments and cursing if you follow your desires. Deuteronomy 28:1–2 (AMP) says,

> If you will listen diligently to the voice of the Lord your God, being watchful to do all His commandments which I command you this day, the Lord your God will set you high above all the nations of the earth. And all these blessings shall come upon you and overtake you if you heed the voice of the Lord your God.

John the Baptist preached repentance for the kingdom of God is coming. Jesus taught and gave parables about the kingdom of God. I believe when we obey, we flow under God's blessings. But when we disobey, we flow under Satan's curse. The best example is in Mark 11:23–26 (KJV), which states,

> For verily I say unto you, That whosoever shall say unto this mountain, Be thou removed,

and be thou cast into the sea; and shall not doubt in his heart, but shall believe [hope— positive expectation] that those things which he saith shall come to pass; he shall have whatsoever he saith. Therefore I say unto you, What things soever ye desire, when ye pray, believe that ye receive them, and ye shall have them. And when ye stand praying, forgive, if ye have ought against any: that your Father also which is in heaven may forgive you your trespasses. But if ye do not forgive, neither will your Father which is in heaven forgive your trespasses.

The conjunction "and" in the twenty-fifth verse makes forgiveness mandatory to receiving that which you are believing for. I believe we cannot love without forgiveness.

We live in a world where people don't like to be corrected. I believe the more you can receive correction, the more you can receive success. Also, if you can't receive correction, you cannot receive success. Young inner-city students think they can become rappers without receiving correction. I point out that rappers like Snoop Dog didn't know everything about music. They had to learn and be corrected to become successful, and they will have to learn and be corrected as well. God wants to correct you, not control you. Many people think when you try to correct them that you are trying to control them. If I ask a male student to pull up his pants or take off his hat in the school building, as soon as I walk past him, the student will look back to see if I am watching and then pull his pants back down or put his hat back on. If you ask them why they pulled their pants down or put their hat back on, many become defensive and say, "I don't like people telling me what to do!" They think my correcting the way they represent themselves is trying to control them. I tell them that no one came off the streets and became successful without accepting correction.

I began this chapter talking about Deuteronomy chapter 28 the bible talking about blessings and cursing. I believe God wants to perfect us to make us more like Him. Ephesians 5:25-27 "Husbands, love your wives, even as Christ also loved the church, and gave himself for it; 26 That he might sanctify and cleanse it with the washing of water by the word, 27 That he might present it to himself a glorious church, not having spot, or wrinkle, or any such thing; but that it should be holy and without blemish." I believe the washing of water by the word is God using people to perfect us. (Ephesians 5:33 ERV) "But each one of you must love his wife as he loves himself. And a wife must respect her husband." God is a God of relationship. Satan tries to destroy relationships. The ten commandments is for our relationship with people or with God.

MEDITATION

I believe meditation is the key not to make success happen but in letting success happen. Working with the homeless population. I ask questions. How much suffering would you go through if you knew you would eventually succeed? And how much suffering would you go through if you believed that God truly loves you? Again, when I'm going through difficult times, I meditate on, "Yes, Jesus loves me because the Bible tells me so." When we feel loved we believe we are safe. We would go through a lot if we believed that success was on the other side of the pain. We would be willing to deal with the pain if we believed that God loves us. "And we know that all things work together for good to them that love God, to them who are the called according to his purpose" (Romans 8:28 KJV).

What we meditate on or think about we bring about. "A good man out of the good treasure of his heart bringeth forth that which is good, and an evil man out of the evil treasure of his heart bringeth forth that which is evil: for of the abundance of the heart his mouth speaketh" (Luke 6:45 KJV). I believe whatever we have in abundance—whether it is negative or positive—will eventually come out of our mouths. Meditating on God's promises creates more positivity in your heart, which in turn allows you to bring forth more good things. This helps to build more hope. Job believed that God loved him. "Then said his wife unto him, Dost thou still retain thine integrity? curse God, and die. But he said unto her, Thou speakest as one of the foolish women speaketh. What? shall we receive good at the hand of God, and shall we not receive evil? In all this did not Job sin with his lips" (Job 2:9–10 KJV). I translate the last verse to say we trust God in good at the hand of God, and shall we not trust God in evil. Again, I believe the challenges in life come to help us grow in our trust in God.

> Blessed is the man that walketh not in the counsel of the ungodly, nor standeth in the way of sinners, nor sitteth in the seat of the scornful. But his delight is in the law of the Lord; and in his law doth he meditate day and night. And he shall be like a tree planted by the rivers of water, that bringeth forth his fruit in his season; his leaf also shall not wither; and whatsoever he doeth shall prosper. (Psalm 1:1–3 KJV)

Meditating on God's Word is spending time with God. First Corinthians 15:33 (NIV) reads, "Do not be misled: 'Bad company corrupts good character.'" Who we spend time with are the people we allow to influence us. Who is a better influence than God?

The thing we meditate or worry about, whether good or bad, will grow like a tree that produces good or bad in our lives. "Keep this Book of the Law always on your lips; meditate on it day and night, so that you may be careful to do everything written in it. Then you will be prosperous and successful" (Joshua 1:8 NIV). We should meditate on God's Word until it changes our thinking and transforms our mind to "prove what *is* that good, and acceptable, and perfect, will of God" (Romans 12:2 KJV). The enemy tries to make us think that meditating on God's Word all day and night is hard work. But then the enemy speaks to us to try to get us to worry or think negatively all day and night. We are going to talk to ourselves in our minds anyway, so why not us God's Word.

CONCLUSION

Revelation 12:11 (KJV) reads, "And they overcame him by the blood of the Lamb, and by the word of their testimony, and they loved not their lives unto the death." We overcome hopelessness by what we say to ourselves. Revelation 12:19–20 (KJV) According to Ephesians 5:19–20 (KJV), "Speaking to yourselves in psalms and hymns and spiritual songs, singing and making melody in your heart to the Lord; Giving thanks always for all things unto God and the Father in the name of our Lord Jesus Christ." What we say aloud has more power than what we think. Death and life are in the power of the tongue! We overcome our negative thoughts by the blood of Jesus and the words of our testimonies (what we say). We should say, "God did it before; God will do it again. God will do it for me!"

ABOUT THE AUTHOR

Michael Byrd, Ph.D., is an award-winning author and speaker. He holds a Ph.D. in theocentric psychology (Christian counseling), a master's in religious education, and a Bachelor of Arts in physical education with a minor in math. He holds The Texas State Certification Board of Alcohol and Drug Counseling, Certified Prevention Specialists. He is a board-certified belief therapist, marriage and family therapist, and a licensed addiction counselor in belief therapy. Although God has called him to be the pastor of Living Word Global Ministries, he has counseled and taught inner-city students for over forty years.

Printed in the United States
by Baker & Taylor Publisher Services